CUBE
BOOK

11-28-11

CUBE
BOOK

WHITE STAR PUBLISHERS

EDITED BY

VALERIA MANFERTO DE FABIANIS

text by
FABRIZIO FINETTI

editorial coordination
GIADA FRANCIA

graphic design
CLARA ZANOTTI

graphic layout
STEFANIA COSTANZO

text translation
CORINNE COLETTE

captions translation
GLENN DEBATTISTA

© 2007 WHITE STAR S.P.A.
VIA CANDIDO SASSONE, 22-24
13100 VERCELLI – ITALY
WWW.WHITESTAR.IT

• United States. Small ghosts during Halloween.

ISBN 978-88-544-0243-0
REPRINTS:
1 2 3 4 5 6   11 10 09 08 07
Printed in China

CONTENTS

PEOPLE

Foreword

THE MYRIAD OF PEOPLE WHO POPULATE OUR WORLD ARE AN EXPRESSION OF THE CONTRADICTORY NATURE OF HUMANITY: ALL PEOPLE ARE SIMULTANEOUSLY BOTH DIFFERENT AND VERY MUCH ALIKE. EVERY NATION HOSTS AN INCREDIBLE VARIETY OF ETHNIC GROUPS AND CULTURES. SOME PEOPLE – ONLY A FEW MILES APART – ARE SO DIFFERENT FROM EACH OTHER THAT THEY DON'T EVEN SEEM TO BELONG TO THE SAME COUNTRY. THIS ELEGANT VOLUME IS A VOYAGE OF EXPLORATION OF THE HUMAN SOUL IN ALL ITS IMMENSE VARIETY, SEEN IN ITS GREATEST GLORY: JOYFUL FESTIVITIES AND CELEBRATIONS, THE STRENGTH-

• Ireland. Final touches before a wedding ceremony at Trinity College in Dublin.

Foreword

ENING LOVE SEEN IN FAMILIES, THE SPIRITUAL RE-
WARD OF RELIGIOUS TRADITIONS, THE UNDYING
ENERGY OF HOMEMAKING AND CHILD-RAISING –
AND THE VIBRANT PLEASURE PEOPLE HAVE IN SIM-
PLY BEING TOGETHER. ALL THESE HOPES AND HAP-
PINESSES ARE SHARED BY THE PEOPLE OF THE
WORLD IN LOCAL TRADITIONS OFTEN CREATED
THOUSANDS OF YEARS AGO.

Valeria Manferto De Fabianis

17 • India. A picture of a young man who forms part
of the nomad shepherds, the Gujjars.

18-19 • France. A young fisherman repairs his traps in Camargue.

20-21 • China. A seller serves clients in a multicolored market in Kashgar.

Introduction

MORE THAN 2000 YEARS AGO, SOPHOCLES SAID: "WONDERS ARE MANY IN THE WORLD, BUT NONE MORE WONDERFUL THAN MAN" AND "HE HAS TAKEN WORDS AND THOUGHT FROM THIN AIR TO PUT THEM TO HIS SERVICE." THIS EMPHATIC VIEW CLEARLY PUTS MANKIND AT THE TOP OF THE WORLD IN THIS, THE FIRST ANALYSIS OF THE RELATIONSHIP BETWEEN NATURE AND CULTURE. SPREAD ACROSS ALL THE LATITUDES OF OUR PLANET, TODAY MANKIND NUMBERS SEVEN BILLION MEMBERS DIVIDED INTO COUNTLESS PEOPLE, TRIBES AND NATIONS. MANKIND IS COMPRISED OF INDIVIDUALS WHO ARE DIFFERENT IN MANY

Introduction

WAYS INCLUDING SKIN COLOR, LIFESTYLE AND RELIGION. MAN IS CURIOUS, BRILLIANT, CREATIVE AND DESTRUCTIVE, ALL AT THE SAME TIME, AND HE IS ABLE TO PERFORM BOTH EXTRAORDINARY AND TERRIBLE FEATS. HOWEVER, IN THE WORDS OF VICTOR HUGO: "WE ALL COME FROM THE SAME CLAY." ANTHROPOLOGY, IN FACT, TELLS US THAT WE ALL BELONG TO A SINGLE BRANCH OF A YOUNG AND COMPLEX EVOLUTIONARY TREE WHICH PROBABLY HAD ITS FIRST BUDS IN AFRICA. OUR EVOLUTION IS CERTAIN ALTHOUGH, NOT KNOWING THE EXACT PATH IT TOOK, WE'RE OBLIGED TO RE-EXAMINE IT EVERY DAY. TODAY, HOWEVER, WE DO SO WITH AN AWARENESS THAT WE ARE NOT THE CENTER OF THE WORLD. WE ARE UNSURE, TOO, ABOUT WHETHER TO CONSIDER OURSELVES PART OF A DIVINE PROJECT OR

Introduction

ONLY THE CHILDREN OF CHANCE. WE HAVE DEVELOPED THE CONVICTION THAT WE ARE ONLY A PART OF THE WHOLE UNIVERSE SURROUNDING US, BUT WE STILL IGNORE OUR DESTINY. IF OUR LIVES ARE REALLY ONLY A MATTER OF CHANCE, THE AGREEMENT CHANCE HAS ASSIGNED TO HUMANITY IS THE MOST INTRIGUING AND EXTRAORDINARY ONE IMAGINABLE. THIS IS WHY, IN THE INFINITE RICHNESS OF THE SEA OF OUR FACES AND IN THE GREAT MULTITUDE OF OUR ACTIONS, WE MAINTAIN TRACES OF OUR PAST WHICH ARE SEEN BOTH IN THE INNOCENCE OF A BABY'S SMILE AND IN THE COMPLEX LABYRINTH OF OUR BEHAVIOR. IN THE DEPTHS OF OUR EYES, WE ARE TRANSFIXED BY THE MYSTERIES OF OUR ANCESTORS WHO SAT AT "BIZARRE GAMING TABLES PLAYING THE GAME OF LIFE."

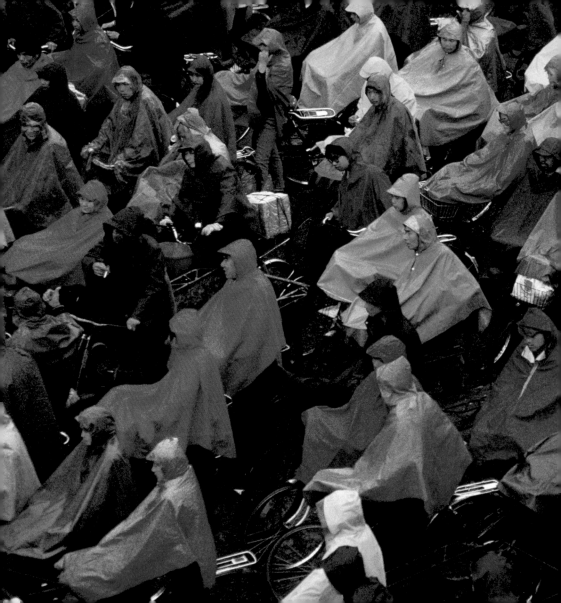

The FACES of MAN

Morocco. A young Berber bride, veiled and ready for her wedding day, with her cheeks rouged in the traditional red spots.

INTRODUCTION The Faces of Man

IF WE WERE TO PAINT A PORTRAIT OF HUMANKIND ON A GIGANTIC CANVAS, WE WOULD FIND OURSELVES IN FRONT OF A POLYCHROME PAINTING DONE WITH FRESH BRUSHSTROKES. IT WOULD BE AN ABSTRACT WORK AND WOULD LOOK MUCH LIKE MODERN ART, BUT IT WOULD REST ON THE ANCIENT CRUST OF THE EARTH. IT WOULD BE A DYNAMIC COMPOSITION WITH THE DIFFERENT SECTIONS COMPRISED OF THE POPULATIONS OF THE WORLD. SOME OF THEM WOULD BE EXPRESSED IN HUGE BLOTCHES OF COLOR WHILE OTHERS WOULD BE REDUCED TO MINUS-CULE AND ALMOST INVISIBLE DOTS. IT WILL NOT SURPRISE YOU TO KNOW THAT 40% OF THE WORLD'S POPULATION IS CHINESE OR INDIAN WHILE DOZENS OF OTHER ETHNIC GROUPS ARE ONLY COMPRISED OF A FEW HUNDRED – AT

INTRODUCTION The Faces of Man

MOST A FEW THOUSAND – MEMBERS. "PEOPLE" "RACES" AND "ETHNIC GROUPS" ARE JUST WORDS THAT AREN'T EVEN THAT IMPORTANT. WHAT IS IMPORTANT, HOWEVER, IS THE INCREDIBLE RANGE OF DIVERSITY WE ARE BLESSED WITH. THE PORTRAIT OF HUMANKIND CAN ALSO BE COMPARED TO AN ANCIENT, CLASSICAL MOSAIC WHICH IS SADLY LOSING SOME OF ITS TILES, WHILE OTHERS ARE BETTER ABLE TO WITHSTAND THE TEST OF TIME AND THE NEW EXIGENCIES OF LIFE. THESE TILES ARE STRONGER AND MORE OVERPOWERING AND THEY STAND OUT CLEARLY IN THIS SCENARIO OF RAPID CHANGE. THE DIFFERENCES WHICH CHARACTERIZE THE MEMBERS OF MANKIND ARE EXCITING, AND THIS RICH DIVERSITY IS BEST EXPRESSED IN OUR EYES WHICH CONCENTRATE THE SMALL UNIVERSE CREATED BY

The Faces of Man
Introduction

EVERY INDIVIDUAL. A SINGLE GENE DETERMINES OUR SKIN COLOR WHILE OTHER, ALMOST INVISIBLE, THREADS LEAD US IN ONE DIRECTION INSTEAD OF ANOTHER. SOME PEOPLE CHOOSE TO HIDE THEIR KNOWLEDGE WHILE OTHERS ARE IMPATIENT TO IMPOSE THEIR CULTURE. SOME PEOPLE HIDE THEIR FACIAL FEATURES BY PAINTING THEIR FACES TO SEDUCE THEIR MATE OR TO SCARE THEIR ENEMY. SOME OF US CONTINUE THE TRADITION OF OUR NOMAD HERITAGE, WHILE OTHERS OPT FOR A SEDENTARY LIFE IN A CITY. SOME PLACE THEIR BETS ON TECHNOLOGY, WHILE OTHERS BELIEVE IN TRADITION. MANY PEOPLE HAVE TO STRUGGLE TO SURVIVE, WHILE OTHERS DISPLAY GREAT WEALTH.

China. A young girl of the Longhorn Miao Tribe poses in her traditional costume.

38 • Japan. An elaborate, traditional hairstyle characterizes this bride
inside a Shinto temple in Tokyo.

39 • Japan. A bride wears a long white kimono which is fastened on the front
and has her head covered by a large hood on her wedding day.

● Japan. A family photo depicts the newlyweds and their relatives in their traditional clothes at the end of the Shinto wedding ceremony.

• Japan. Parents and children wearing colorful kimonos take part in a traditional Japanese celebration.

China. Intensity and sweetness can be read in the eyes of this elderly man in Kashgar in the region of Sinkiang.

● China. A young boy peeps out from behind a photography-shop door in Kashgar, Sinkiang.

China. A row of young students write their teacher's dictation in Guangxi, Southern China.

50 • China. Photo of an elderly woman, of Yi ethnicity, carrying a load of hay in the province of Yunnan.

51 • China. In the rural village of Turpan, an Uighur farmer happily carries his wheat crop.

52 • China. The pride of age on the face of a woman of the Hakka tribe in the village of Kam Tin.

53 • China. In Yangshuo in the autonomous region of Zhuang, an elderly man smokes a pipe.

54 • China. A Lahu girl from the province of Yunnan, grants
a smile to the camera.

55 • China. A Miao child proudly showing his traditional costume, enriched
by a headdress and a large silver medallion, appears at the window.

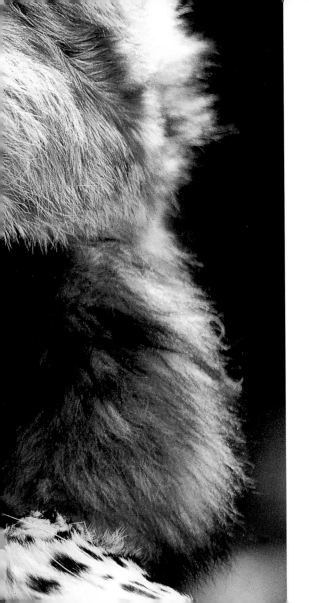

● China. Two representatives of
the Khampa nomad people who
live on the plateau in the Tibetan
region of Kham, at 14764 ft
(4500 m).

India. A cascade of turquoise adorns the hairstyle of a young Ladakh girl. The clothes and the precious jewelry form part of the girl's dowry.

60 • China. The serene gaze of a Tibetan girl wearing a traditional headdress, quilted with pearls and stones of varying value.

61 • China. In Tibet men also like to adorn themselves. According to Buddhist tradition, jewels indicate the social status and the spiritual level of those who wear them.

India. The Perak, a traditional leather hat of the Himalayan Ladakh populations, is worn by both males and females.

64 • Nepal. A small girl poses shyly on the doorstep of her house.

65 • Nepal. The excuse of a photo grants a short break for a young girl.

66 • India. In Rajasthan turbans are an essential part of male attire: it is calculated that there are over a thousand different ways of binding these typical Indian headdresses.

67 • India. A man proudly shows the peculiar style of his moustache and beard.

● India. A Gujjar farmer on a pilgrimage grants himself a moment of repose at a hostel in Pushkar, a sacred city of Rajasthan.

India. A Rajasthan girl, veiled with a finely decorated red sari, carries a basket on her head. In her intense close-up picture (right) it is possible to recognize her intention of looking like the model dictated by the goddess Parvati, consort of Shiva and venerated by married women.

India. The tikala are painted on the forehead of two Rajasthan ascetics. These are marks which declare their identity and the sect of which they form part of.

● Indonesia. A Minangkabau girl poses on a Rumah Gadang window before her wedding. The bride wears an elegant red dress with an elaborate hairdo and precious jewels.

Vietnam. A picture taken of village
women during a celebration.

78 • Vietnam. A sincere smile illuminates the face of a Vietnamese man.

79 • Vietnam. The elaborate hairstyle of a Vietnamese woman uses colorful ribbons and fabric to hold her long, black hair.

80 • Vietnam. Three girls pose and smile during Tet, the Vietnamese New Year.

81 • Vietnam. A girl's simple make-up highlight the tints of the colorful flowers which are the perfumed fulcrum of many Vietnamese feasts, particularly Tet.

Thailand. The primeval elegance of two "giraffe" women of the Padaung tribe, who are wearing heavy brass-coil neck rings.

84 • Thailand. Two embracing girls acquiesce to have their picture taken as a memento.

85 • Thailand. The sweet smile of a girl from Bangkok.

86 • Bhutan. Four children smile behind
a window in Thimphu.

86-87 • Burma. A young monk looks out
of the door of the Shwenandaw monastery,
also called "The Golden Palace."

88 ● Bhutan. Traditional headdresses are utilized by women during their work and celebrations.

89 ● Bhutan. Gold and turquoise earrings and a necklace of pearls and gemstones: in keeping with tradition, this woman is wearing jewelry that symbolizes virtue and spirituality.

● Bhutan. A smile, the result of a deep serenity, illuminates the faces of two elderly people.

92-93 • Niger. A young Bororo (or Wodaabe) wears a traditional cone-shaped straw hat adorned with ostrich feathers over his white headdress.

93 • Niger. The Bororo tribe are, in their daily life, very meticulous about their outward appearance – in the photo the girl is wearing a traditional dress and colored necklaces.

94 • Egypt. A young Bedouin girl from the peninsula of Sinai holds a green headscarf with her teeth in order to cover her face.

95 • Mauritania. Close up of a girl of the Nomad Tuaregh tribe, in the Sahara desert, as she covers her face with her hand.

Nigeria. Red turbans emphasize the dignity of the impassive guardsmen of the Nigerian Emir of Kano.

Egypt. The female clothes used by the Bedouin tribes conform to the dictates of Islam, which prescribe the use of veils for adult women. Some wear the Hijab on their face, a colored fabric decorated with pendants of various shapes.

Mali. The Tagelmust is the characteristic turban of the Tuaregh, usually blue in color. It protects the face from the sun and the sand carried by the desert wind.

● Ethiopia. Amongst the tribes
which live in the valley of the Omo
River there are the Mursi, with their
faces painted in white fossil lime.
They wear horns as headdresses
and utilize the custom of wearing lip
and ear plates.

104 • Nigeria. The tattoo-decorated face and the head decorated with braids belong
to a Fulani shepherd, part of nomadic tribe widespread in the entire African Sahelian zone.

105 • Nigeria. A woman with the typical female hairstyle employed by the Fulani
with beads and fabrics intertwined in her hair.

Tanzania. The aesthetic sense of the Masai women is revealed in the extremely elaborate ornaments, nowadays composed with an infinite number of plastic beads.

Kenya. A photo of the elegant figure of two Masai, the proud nomads that live on the southern plains of the country.

110 • Ethiopia. A child, photographed near the Termaber pass, wears a straw headdress and a turban to protect him from the wind.

111 • South Africa. A Xhosa girl's smile in Johannesburg. The Xhosas are one of the most important ethnic groups in South Africa.

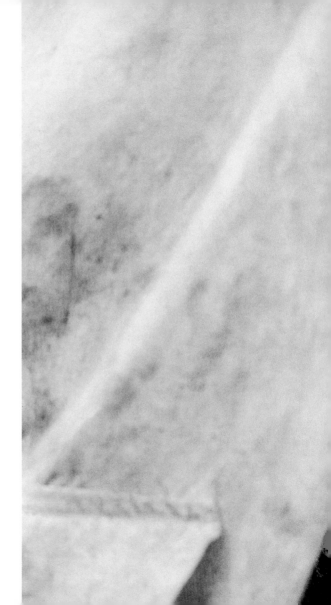

Russia. A Chukchi farmer drinks a warm beverage inside his tent in the inhospitable Siberian Northeastern Taiga.

114 ● Kazakhstan. Four mounted
hunters are about to free their
golden eagles.

114-115 ● Kazakhstan.
A hunter pets his
inseparable eagle.

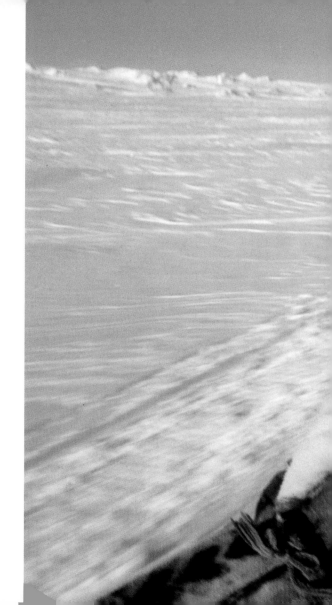

● United States.
A Inuit child aboard a
sleigh in Alaska wears a
caribou-fur coat in the
icy expanse of the
Alaskan arctic.

118 • Sweden. Three children from Stockholm reveal their different origins with a smile.

119 • Russia. White snow frames the face of a child from Moscow.

Finland. The fresh and simple beauty of three Scandinavian girls. Young Finns are usually informal in their attire and hairstyles.

122 • Ireland. Two students practice hurling on the turf in Kilkenny.

123 • Ireland. The seriousness of the school uniforms contrasts with the laughter of some young students of Kilkenny.

● Ireland. The innocent smile of two young boys of the emerald isle.

126 • United States. The Zion Park in Utah becomes, for this boy, a fantastic place, ideal for play.

127 • Sweden. A girl in traditional attire has her photo taken, in Skansen, Stockholm.

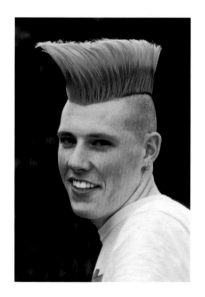

Great Britain. In London it is easy to find
any type of fashion trend.

130 • Italy. The proud look of an inhabitant of Barbagia, who is wearing a traditional Sardinian costume.

131 • Greece. Dusk light sculpts the face of this elderly man in Chania, on the island of Crete.

132 • Ireland. An impromptu photo of two friends on the threshold of a tavern in Belleek.

133 • Greece. On the streets of Athens, an old man is completely absorbed as he reads his newspaper.

ΑΠΟΓΕΥΜΑΤΙΝΗ

θα σκότωναν ακόμη και παιδιά με Ι.Χ.- τορπίλη

20

Ξένους διπλωμάτες είχαν στόχο αυτή τη φορά οι τρομοκράτες

ΒΗΡΥΤΟ ΕΚΑΝΑΝ ΤΗΝ ΑΘΗΝΑ

Κοκκίνισε και το Κύπελλο

Επτά τραυμάτισε η τηλεκατευθυνόμενη
Κινδύνεψε κι ο πρώην Πρόεδρος

ΜΟΝΟ ΣΤΗΝ "Α"
Αυξάνουν
50% Τα

Denmark. A satisfied-looking sailor in Skagen, in the southern county of Jutland.

136 • Ireland. A bench in front of the Grand Canal in Dublin is the ideal place
to rest and smoke a pipe.

137 • Ireland. In modern Dublin it is still possible to find a conservative soul represented
by the pipe and bowler worn by this gentleman.

Ireland. The famous equestrian contest, the Royal Dublin Horse Show is also
a very important social event: on the right, two judges take a walk
on the lawn whilst a spectator (top) watches the competitions.

Ireland. Little gluttons enjoy various types of sweets as they sit on the threshold of a public place or lean against an attractive bakery window.

142 • United States. In Seneca, Oregon, a cowboy holds his faithful horse with a bridle.

143 • United States. Horse and trainer look out from the window of a stable in Wyoming.

• French Polynesia. Ample straw hats and colorful clothes characterize these women who are sitting on churches pews, during a mass in Papeete.

146-147 ● Cuba.
A timeless photo of
a musician walking
in the street.

148-149 ● Bolivia.
Aymara women gather
at Copacabana for a
traditional Bolivian feast.
They are wearing
bowler hats, a custom
introduced by the
British during the
construction of the
Andean railway.

Peru. Proud of their animals, the inhabitants of an Andean village pose while wearing traditional clothes.

152 • Ecuador. Whorls of colored wool protect a young child from the cold in the mountain villages.

153 • Peru. The profile of a girl with a traditional bowler hat.

154-155 • Peru. Like a mirror image, two women deriving from the region of Cuzco offer us the same smile.

LIVING DWELLINGS

Ivory Coast. The Baule inhabitants of an artisan village in Mekro look upwards and are immortalized in a moment of daily life.

INTRODUCTION Living Dwellings

ONE DEFINITION SEES THE HOME AS: "THE RESULT OF OPERATIONS THROUGH WHICH MAN TRANSFORMS A PART OF THE NATURAL ENVIRONMENT INTO A SHELTER FOR HIMSELF AND HIS FAMILY," AND GOES ON TO SAY THAT THE HOME, "TAKES ON DIFFERENT SHAPES AND CHARACTERISTICS ACCORDING TO THE EXTENT OF THE DEVELOPMENT OF A CIVILIZATION AND OF ITS ENVIRONMENTAL AND CLIMATIC CHARACTERISTICS." THESE CONSTANTS ARE STRICTLY LINKED TO HUMAN LIFE. THE HOME, THEREFORE, IS THE RESULT OF A TRANSFORMATION BY MAN OF THE SPACE HE USES FOR CARRYING OUT HIS VITAL FUNCTIONS. IT IS AN ELEMENT OF CONTINUITY OR, BETTER YET, AN EXPANSION OF THE INDIVIDUAL AND COLLECTIVE PERSONALITY. IN FACT, HUMANKIND HAS LIVED IN THIS SORT OF NAT-

INTRODUCTION Living Dwellings

URAL SYMBIOSIS FOR THOUSANDS OF YEARS, BUILDING "HORIZONTAL CIVILIZATIONS" WHERE HOMES, VILLAGES AND CITIES WERE A SIMPLE CONCENTRATION OF THE SURROUNDING ENVIRONMENT. THE SPECTACULAR RESULTS WERE AN INTIMATE CONNECTION BETWEEN MAN AND THE MATERIALS AVAILABLE TO HIM. BUT TODAY, WE CLEARLY LIVE IN A "VERTICAL CIVILIZATION." UBIQUITOUSLY, BLOCKS OF STONE AND SLABS OF ICE, ALONG WITH DRIED MANURE AND MUD HAVE SERVED TO CREATE RATIONAL AND WELCOMING SHAPES TO PROTECT AND THERMALLY INSULATE MAN FROM HIS ENVIRONMENT, BUT ALSO TO IRREVOCABLY CONNECT HIM TO IT. MAN HAS BEEN ABLE TO SKILLFULLY DESIGN EXTRAORDINARY ARCHITECTURE AND TO COPY PERFECT SHAPES FROM NATURE TO CREATE SUP-

Living Dwellings

Introduction

PLE WOODEN AND METAL STRUCTURES. HE HAS ALSO IN-VENTED NEW MATERIALS AND CAST WAVES OF STEEL TO BUILD HIS HOMES AND IMBUE THEM WITH HIS OWN IDENTI-TY. HE DOES THIS TO REAFFIRM A CONCEPT OF LIFE AND TO GIVE FREE REIN TO HIS BOUNDLESS CREATIVITY. THE HOME IS A SYMBOL FOR EVERYONE, FOR THOSE WHO HAVE CHOSEN A SEDENTARY LIFESTYLE AND EVEN FOR THE NOMAD. HOMES CAN BE IMMENSE AND SUMPTUOUS LIKE ROYAL RESIDENCES IN MANY PARTS OF THE WORLD OR CAN SIMPLY BE A GROUPING OF THREE STONES, AS IS THE CASE FOR THE TURKANA PEOPLE, WHO ALWAYS HAVE A HEARTHSTONE AND WHO BUILD THEIR LIVES AROUND IT.

- Canada. In the arctic regions, tents are created by tying the skins of caribous, the same animal that serves the Inuit to protect their bodies from the region's low temperatures.

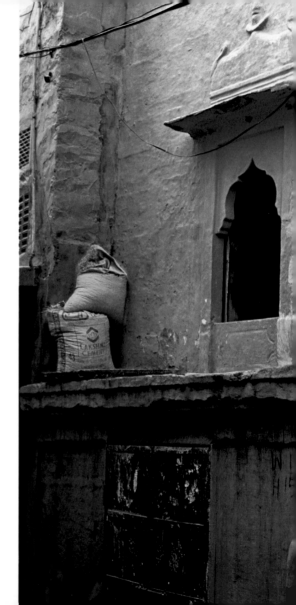

India. In Rajasthan, main doors are often placed at an upper level rather than on the street, almost as if to indicate that the house is a place of retreat, both spiritual and material, from daily social interaction.

● India. Colors have an important significance for several populations and therefore the walls of a house in Rajasthan acquire a precise value according to the choice made.

● India. The finely decorated doors
and windows of the historical dwellings
of Jaisalmer in Rajasthan denote
the Indian culture's taste for detail.

• South Korea.
Very old houses
posses a bright
internal courtyard with
a small garden, an ideal
place for contact
with nature within
domestic walls.

170 • Japan. House care is assigned to women within the Japanese tradition.

170-171 • Japan. The ritual of tea is lived both as a religious moment, as a contemplation, and as an act of hospitality.

172 • China. The building of a house, like this in Longji, can be a social event in which many families participate.

172-173 • China. A young woman wearing festive attire looks out of the window of a traditional Zhuang house.

174 • Nepal. Two children play on a stone wall in a village in Kathmandu.

175 • Nepal. Sitting on their doorsteps near a yak, time flies by for the two boys in a village where the pace of life is incomparable to that of the Western world.

India. The Himalayan houses in Ladakh are practically devoid of windows in order to better resist the rigid winter temperatures. The inhabitants live a life which has remained the same through the years and the centuries.

178-179 and 179 ● India. The long and comfortable floating houses of Srinagar, in Kashmir, are an excellent solution when facing the rigid winter in these latitudes.

180-181 ● China. The dokpa tent, of Mongol origin, is composed of dismountable wooden elements and felt carpets.

182-183 ● Turkey. The shepherds' stone and brick houses, emerge like small natural hills amongst the green pastures of Harran.

● Russia. The Yaranga is a large tent constituted of a framework of poles intertwined at the top, covered with reindeer hide. The stone circle used to secure it is a characteristic feature.

Ciad. A nomad returns home at dusk in his hemispherical-shaped tent, in the margins of an endless expanse of sand.

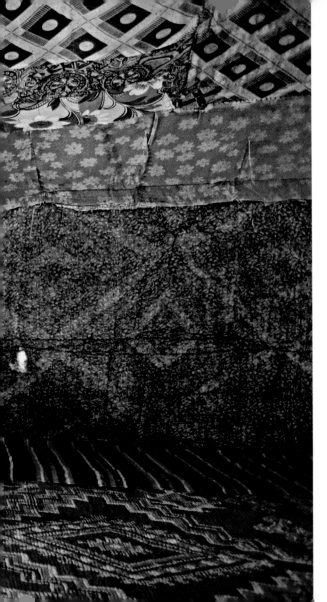

188-189 ● Algeria. Albeit comfortable and richly decorated, a tent is the only dwelling which the nomad populations of the Sahara can afford.

190-191 ● Tunisia. The large black tents in Tuaregh, which respond to precise logistic necessities, are made of goat skin and covered with black clay.

192 • Egypt. Besides water, which allows extensive agriculture, the large Nile provides the inhabitants, who live along its shores with materials to build their homes.

193 • Egypt. A family stops near the door of a house on the shore of the Nile in the vicinity of Luxor.

194 and 194-195 • Mauritania. The Berber houses, built in the borders of the large Sahara desert, satisfy the spiritual needs of the inhabitants, besides granting them protection from the intolerable desert temperatures.

196-197 • Ethiopia. In the early afternoon a girl looks out of her hut door in the village of Omorate in the Omo Valley.

198 • Kenya. A young Masai woman weaves the dry branches which will constitute
her new hut's roof.

199 • Kenya. A Turkana woman is completing the building of a hut. During the rainy season
a terracotta vase, fastened with strips of skin, is placed on the top of the roof.

200 • South Africa. An artist completes the decorations on the wall of a house in Botshabelo.

201 • South Africa. In Mabhoko, the halls of historical houses are decorated with geometric figures painted in glaring colors.

Peru.
The combinations of
colors emphasize
the solar aspect of
Trujillo's colonial
architecture.

Cuba. A refined eclecticism combined with an innate sense of color, give life to evocative and unique decorations on the walls of houses.

206-207 and 207 • United States. Generous bunches of red peppers adorn the balconies and windows on the occasion of the Hatch Chile Festival, in New Mexico.

208-209 • Italy. A man returns home after a day in the fields in Alberobello. The huts are built with superimposed bricks, which result in the characteristic conical roof.

210-211 • Italy. The light of dusk creates a dreamlike atmosphere grazing the huts' rooftops.

212 and 213 ● United Kingdom. The system of covering and finishing thatched roofs
follows a traditional method handed down for thousands of years.

214-215 ● Ireland. Seen from above, this traditional house of Celtic origin
in Inishmore takes on the shape of a vessel lost in the greenery.

216 • Ireland. Once, many doors had brass knockers like this one.

216-217 • Ireland. The vivaciously colored doors and shutters were one of the few ornaments allowed by the rigid rules of Georgian architecture.

218-219 • France. An unusual perspective unites highlights a moment of intimacy caught in the interior of a mansard, with the *par excellence* symbol of Paris in the background.

United States. The American flags color the doorways of cottages on the occasion of a national anniversary in Oak Bluffs, Massachusetts.

United States. The memories of a life at sea decorate the main façade of this house in Massachusetts.

224 • Italy. A farmer looks out of the door of his maso in Val di Funes in Trentino Alto Adige.

224-225 • United States. The choice of living isolated in an isolated cottage on the borders of Canada represents, for some Americans, the desire to return to the origins of their nation.

Canada. The Inuit tent,
covered in caribou skins, has a fire
lit on the steatite (soapstone) in
the center, the only source
of light and heat.

Greenland. To finish an igloo's roof one needs to know how to skillfully work ice using a long sharp knife.

• Canada. Once built, the igloo must be covered in fresh snow to strengthen and insulate the structure.

PEOPLE and PROFESSIONS

India. A woman carries out her work as she hangs up huge,
colored drapes in a laundry.

INTRODUCTION People and Professions

Love and work, according to Freud, are the great driving forces of human life because they place man in real situations. They give meaning and importance to his existence and provide confirmation of his value and role in society. Since the beginning of time, we have recognized that work has the power to shape the world and the individual lives involved. Work has accompanied man since his origins and it is something which cannot be separated from his own inner nature: they are linked by his need to survive and to cultivate and transform the earth. All societies and political systems are based

INTRODUCTION People and Professions

ON WORK AND EVEN THE GREAT RELIGIONS, IN-
SPIRED BY THE BELIEF IN AN ACT OF CREATION BY A
SUPERIOR BEING, TRANSMIT TO US THE CONCEPT
OF THE FIRST, INCREDIBILE DIVINE GENERATION. HU-
MAN ACTIVITIES ARE INFINITE: EVERY DAY, NEW
JOBS ARE CREATED WHILE OTHERS DISAPPEAR. IN
THE MEANTIME, BILLIONS OF MEN ARE BUSY
TRANSFORMING THE SURFACE OF OUR PLANET OR
JUST REPEATING ANCIENT ACTS REQUIRED IN OR-
DER TO SUPPORT THEMSELVES AND THEIR FAMI-
LIES. WORK CAUSES MIGRATIONS – OF SINGLE INDI-
VIDUALS AND OF ENTIRE PEOPLES – AND THIS IS A
CAUSE AND EFFECT OF RICHNESS, POVERTY AND
EXPLOITATION. THESE PHOTOS – WHETHER

People and Professions
Introduction

POIGNANT BECAUSE OF THEIR PROFOUND BEAUTY OR DISTURBING BECAUSE OF THE HARSHNESS THEY EVOKE – ENTER OUR LIVES AND PROFESSIONAL WORLD AND INSTANTLY TAKE US TO FARAWAY SITUATIONS. MAN'S HANDS AND HIS WILL ARE THE ABSOLUTE PROTAGONISTS BECAUSE MAN IS MALLEABLE AND SENSITIVE AND ABLE TO OVERCOME IMPOSSIBLE CHALLENGES OVER AND OVER AGAIN. IN THE END, WE ARE FORCED TO REALIZE THAT LIFE, FROM THE VERY MOMENT OF CONCEPTION IS, IN ITSELF, AN INFINITE AND MYSTERIOUS WORK WHICH OCCUPIES US UNTIL WE DIE.

237 ● France. A laborer, protected by a masked helmet, works in a furniture factory.

238-239 ● Ireland. The delivery of beer kegs is the indispensable prelude to a long evening in the pub.

France. Owners and managers of popular pubs in Montmartre, Paris, take care of their businesses in anticipation of the usual waves of patrons.

China. The vertiginous rhythm of national economic growth in Shanghai. The construction imposes an irreversible transformation onto the urban landscape.

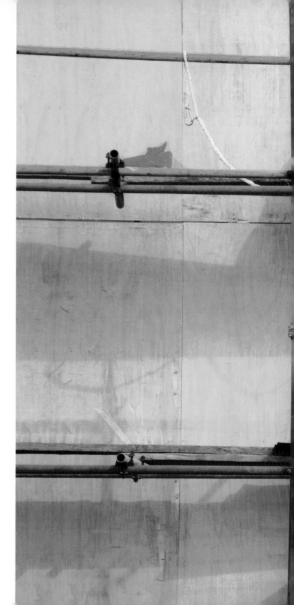

244 • United Arab Emirates. Some workers are finishing the construction of the minaret of a new mosque in Dubai.

244-245 • China. Suspended on high scaffolds, some workers are completing the external plastering of a building.

246-247 ● China. Red is definitely the most valued color in the production of these enormous traditional fans.

248-249 ● Thailand. A worker fastens the screws on the planks that are destined to become a trawler.

250 and 251 • France. Part acrobat and part artiste, Marseille's shipyard workers finish their paint work on the flanks of two boats.

252-253 • Brazil. The repair of a boat which has to confront the ocean's waves is a work to be performed with love and patience.

254-255 ● Ireland.
Three sailors bring their
boat to shore after
having been out at sea.

256-257 ● Scotland.
An old sailor prepares a
cage for catching
lobsters.

England. Beside the usual hard work, fishermen have to face both the risks and the devastating force of the stormy sea.

260-261 • France. An ocean trawler's sailors divide the caught fish, picking out the varieties that will be more profitable on the market.

262-263 • Sri Lanka. The type of fishing adopted along the southern coasts of the island is one of the most spectacular methods that exist of this ancient and noble art.

264-265 • Myanmar. In perfect synchronization, two Intha fishermen throw their fish-traps into the waters of the Inle lake.

Nigeria. Thousands of fishermen crowd the Fishing Festival at Argungo, on the shores of the Sokoto river. The participants try to catch fish with their bare hands or with small nets, helped only by a turnip acting as a buoy.

268-269 ● Tanzania. Algae harvesting represents an important part in the domestic economy of thousands of people in Zanzibar.

269 ● Mozambique. Some sailors throw their nets near the shore during the daily fishing.

India. For those who live on the seaside, purchasing fish is often an event that occurs as the boats return to shore with a catch.

Japan. Like immense boulders, hundreds of large tuna wait to be sold at Tokyo's fish market.

274 and 274-275 ● South Africa. Mining work in the bowels of the earth is certainly one of the most difficult and dangerous human activities in existence.

276-277 ● China. The hard work of a foundry reminds man of the unending process of the transformation of matter.

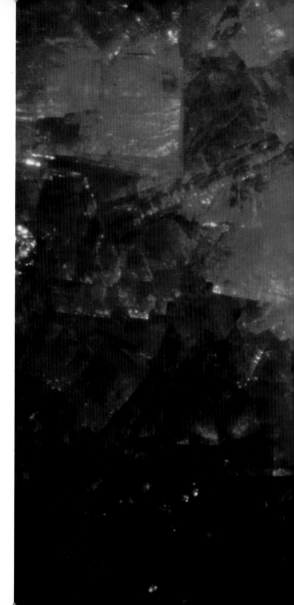

278-279 ● Canada. The blacksmith's ancient craft requires considerable strength and precision skills.

279 ● Great Britain. Holding the animal's foot with great force, a blacksmith starts to fit a horse with horseshoes.

280 • Turkey. Mat and carpet weaving is not
always a female prerogative.

281 • Morocco. With skillful and rapid movements, a woman weaves
a woolen carpet in a village of the Mgoun valley.

282-283 ● India. In precarious balance on a large wooden grate, a woman hangs recently-dyed, colorful saris, out to dry.

284-285 ● Morocco. A man pours a bucket of red pigment in the popular dyers quarter of Marrakech.

285 ● Morocco. A dyer, swamped by his load, carries large coils of red spun wool towards the souk (marketplace).

286-287 ● Morocco. Because of its acid emanations, the multicolored quarter of Fez is more reminiscent of an infernal tract rather than a work place.

288-289 ● Morocco. Sheep and goats' skins are the primary resources utilized by the skillful artisans of the tanners' quarter of Fez.

● Afghanistan. A motley group of adults and youths attends lessons in an improvised classroom, sheltered by a large tent, inside a ditch.

292-293 • Holland. In this barber shop which has maintained its original décor one breathes an old-fashioned atmosphere.

293 • Cuba. In Havana, the barber's profession can be practiced on a stool under the arches of a porch.

294 • Belgium. An elderly barber trims a client's mustache with extreme care.

295 • China. In Pamir, shaving with a sharp razor called "straighù" provokes a grimace of pain from the unfortunate client.

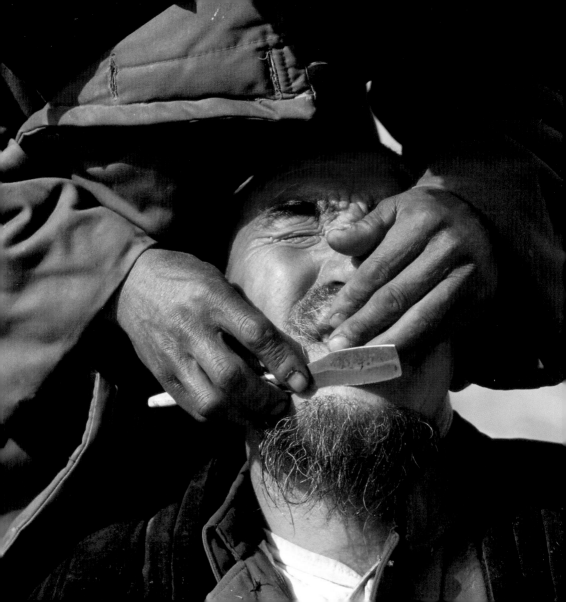

India. Cattle markets in Rajasthan are an important meeting place for the men of the surrounding villages.

298-299 ● Vietnam. Keeping a short distance, a man leads his geese to pasture.

300-301 ● India. A very rigid climate and an often arid territory, make sheep farming very hard work in the Himalayan region of Ladakh.

China. Milking animals is a female task in Tibetan society.

304 • United States. The lasso is an indispensable tool for the modern cowboy.

305 • United States. Two cowboys lead a herd towards a ranch in Wyoming.

306-307 • Norway. The survival of the Sami people is still tightly bound
to the herding of reindeers.

308-309 • Ethiopia.
A group of rigorously
trained Konso women
carry their heavy load
of wood, gathered in
the forest, back to
the village.

310-311 • China.
Along the Brahmaputra,
in Tibet, even the
steepest terrains
is used for the
cultivation of millet,
which is gathered in
baskets and carried
down to the plain.

• Vietnam. Rice field work, indispensable for the survival of the country, is very often still devoid of any form of mechanization.

314 • India. In some of the country's regions, fishing is undertaken for the benefit of the community and not for personal profit.

315 • India. Immersed up to her ankles in a rice field, an elderly woman tries to fish with the use of a special basket used as a fish trap.

316-317 ● Japan. Almost submerged by enormous green pillows, three women start the gathering of leaves in a tea plantation.

317 ● Sri Lanka. The long working day does not erase a young tea gatherer's smile.

318-319 ● India. A group of women carry the precious load, just gathered from a tea plantation, on their heads.

Yemen. A group
of women, pictured
while working in the fields
in Hadhramaut (left), are wearing
the *madhallè*, the characteristic
pointed straw hat.

● Cuba. Tobacco cultivation and manufacturing are one of the most important traditional resources of the island and require long and accurate care.

324-325 • Peru. In order to eliminate weeds, a group of workers shovel, in perfect synchronization, a large camp of potatoes.

326-327 • France. The sunny and perfumed work of lavender cultivators in Provence.

328-329 ● Vietnam. Whilst protecting herself from the sun with the popular pointed hat, a woman checks as thousands of candies dry out in Saigon.

330-331 ● Pakistan. The selection and desiccation of apricots is a process entirely done by women.

India. The immense quantities of cotton that are harvested in the south of the country give life, albeit for short periods, to real fairy-tale like visions.

Thailand. Extracted from deep mines or obtained from large saltworks, salt reminds man of one of the most ancient trades in history.

336 ● Guatemala. Colorful flower markets regularly occupy the steps of many churches.

337 ● Guatemala. A picture of the famous and crowded market of Chichicastenango.

India. A trader, in Rajasthan, neatly arranges the colorful sweets on his market stall whilst another one arranges large baskets of roses used as offerings from the faithful.

• Vietnam. During market day, the only time available to stop for lunch is when there is a lull in the flow of customers.

Vietnam. Boats loaded with every type of product swarm the market of Phung Hiep in the delta of the Mekong river.

Philippines. While adults organize the goods, a young seashell and coral seller grants himself a brief moment of rest.

A WORLD of LOVE

The Bahamas. A tender kiss between mother and daughter attests to the deep love which binds them.

INTRODUCTION A World of Love

ALL OF US, OFTEN UNCONSCIOUSLY, MEANDER DAILY THROUGH THE MOST COMPLEX AND MYSTERIOUS DYNAMICS IN EXISTENCE: FAMILY RELATIONSHIPS, PARTICULARLY THOSE BETWEEN CHILDREN AND PARENTS. IN OPENING A BOOK, WHICH WAS WRITTEN TO PROVIDE GUIDANCE TO PARENTS, THESE DEFINITIONS STAND OUT: "THE FAMILY IS THE FOCUS OF A RELATIONSHIPS WHICH MAKES IT POSSIBLE FOR EACH OF ITS MEMBERS TO CARRY ON WITH THEIR OWN LIVES ON ALL LEVELS, INCLUDING THE BIOLOGICAL AND CULTURAL ONES. THE FAMILY IS A PLACE WHERE RELATIONSHIPS ARE NECESSARY FOR THE FULL REALIZATION OF ONE'S SELF." THIS IS A POSITIVE AND HELPFUL DEFINITION WHICH I FULLY AGREE WITH. IN FACT, THE FAMILY

INTRODUCTION A World of Love

IS THE FABRIC AND THE LIFE OF EVERY MAN IS EN-
TWINED IN ITS WEAVE. IT IS MUCH MORE IMPORTANT
THAN A SENSELESS LIST OF PRIORITIES (SUCCESS,
MONEY, FAME). THE FAMILY IS, BASICALLY, THE CRE-
ATION OF A COUPLE WHICH, LIKE ANY LIVING ORGAN-
ISM, IS BORN, LIVES AND DIES. FAMILIES ARE BORN,
GROW AND DISSOLVE EITHER IN A NATURAL OR A
FORCED WAY. FAMILY MEANS HOME, THE PLACE
WHERE OUR IDENTITY UNFOLDS, AND THE SENSE OF
FAMILY IS SOMETHING WHICH ACCOMPANIES US
THROUGHOUT OUR WHOLE LIVES. FOR ALL HUMAN BE-
INGS, FAMILY MEANS ROOTS, PROTECTION, AFFECTION
AND GUIDANCE. CHILDREN ARE THE STARS IN THE FAM-
ILY MICROCOSM. THEY BRING THEIR BEAUTY, ENTHUSI-

A World of Love

ASM, INNOCENCE, SPONTANEITY AND EFFORT TO IT AND GIVE THEIR PARENTS A BOUNDLESS AND UN-EQUALED GIFT. CHILDREN BRING JOY AND PAIN TO THE ADULTS AROUND THEM, SOMETIMES MAKING THEM SMILE AND OTHER TIMES, CRY. MOTHERS AND FATHERS ALL OVER THE WORLD WELCOME THEIR CHILDREN AND DO THEIR BEST TO TEACH AND GUIDE THEM BUT THEY NEVER LOSE THEIR ASTONISHMENT AT THE MIRACLE BEFORE THEM. FAMILY, LASTLY, IS WHERE WE LOOK IN-TO THE EYES OF MOTHER AND FATHER AND FIND THE REAL SIGNIFICANCE OF OUR OWN LIVES.

• Mali. The complete dependence on his mother can be seen in the gaze of this young child.

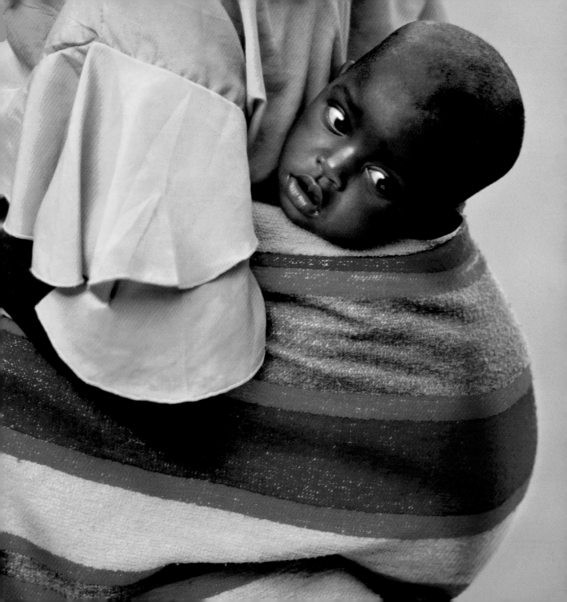

Thailand. A Padaung child admiringly observes her mother who is playing an old wooden guitar.

● Thailand. A little girl
watches as two
women of the
Yao tribe in Chiang Rai
embroider a traditional
costume.

356 • Mongolia. A grandmother takes care of her niece who lays on a traditional cradle.

356-357 • China. A woman's tender smile directed at her newborn little girl in Kasghar.

358 • China. A Tajik mother cradles her son in a typical dry mud house
of the Pamir plateau.

359 • China. Bound to the cradle with a ribbon, the small boy waits for the attentions
of his mother who is intent on preparing a small necklace or trinket.

Kyrghizistan.
A Bulan Seget family
exhibits their beautiful
carpets with the
Tianshan mountains in
the background.

362-363 • India. A Mizo child holds her mother's hand during the celebrations of the Kut festival.

363 • Sweden. A child wearing a traditional costume gets ready for the midsummer celebration in Dalarna.

364-365 • Japan. Accompanied by his parent, a boy attends the Heian Shinto Shrine in Kyoto, a celebration for the young from 3 to 7 years of age.

365 • Japan. A family leads their young daughter to the Heian Shinto Shrine in Kyoto.

366-367 ● Nepal. A family welcome the arrival of a visitor with good-natured smiles.

368-369 ● Peru. In several societies, the unbreakable relationship between mother and child is still strong despite the difficult conditions of life.

370 ● Vietnam. The bicycle is still the only means of travel for many families.

371 ● Thailand. Mother and child move by canoe in the floating market of Damnoen Saduak.

India. Mother and daughters walk in front of the splendid temple of Harmandir Sahib in Amritsar.

374-375 ● Guatemala. A curious serenity seeps from this little boy's gaze in Chichicastenango.

376-377 ● Peru. A young woman, wearing a traditional costume, carries her child in Ollantaytambo.

378-379 ● Kenya. Leaning on one of the tribe-women, a small girl turns her curious gaze towards the photographer.

380 • Senegal. A woman from Dakar turns her loving gaze towards her young son.

381 • Tanzania. The innocent smile of a little girl held tightly to her mother.

382-383 • Niger. A mother nurses her son while others rest in a Tuaregh tent.

384 • Nigeria. A Fulbe woman nurses her son. The Fulani are nomad shepherds from the Sahel area.

385 • Nigeria. Breast feeding has fundamental significance in the development of a mother and child's relationship.

386 • United States. A man imparts the first fishing lesson to his son in Dillon Lake, Colorado.

386-387 • France. Father and son wait for the low tide to fish for prawns on the coast of Bretagne.

388 ● United States. A family spends a serene day strolling in a field.

388-389 ● Germany. Father and son have chosen the flourishing shores near the springs of the Danube in the Bohemian Forest, for a healthy jaunt on their bikes.

390 • Iceland. Sitting on her father's shoulders, a little girl takes part in the celebrations.

391 • Norway. In a moment of relaxation, father and son exchange tender caresses.

392-393 • Switzerland. Tightly held together on board a sleigh, mother and daughter launch themselves towards the snow.

394 • Norway. Taking part in local traditions is a value that is passed on though many communities all over the world.

395 • Norway. A Laplander proudly shows his small son the land where he will live.

The TIME of the SOUL

China. The devotion of a woman lost in prayer in Tashilhunpo, Tibet.

INTRODUCTION The Time of the Soul

THERE IS NO OTHER HUMAN EXPERIENCE AS VAST AND AS PROFOUND AS RELIGIOUS SENTIMENT. HERE, MAN QUESTIONS ALL HIS ACCOMPLISHMENTS AND, IN THIS WAY, CREATES A PATRIMONY RICHER THAN ALL OTHERS. WHAT DOES IT ALL MEAN? AND JUST WHAT IS A SPIRITUAL OR RELIGIOUS EXPERIENCE? PERHAPS THERE WILL NEVER BE A CLEAR ANSWER TO THIS UNIVERSAL QUESTION, BUT IT OBLIGES US TO INVESTIGATE OUR WHOLE EXISTENCE. IT IS EASY TO PLACE RELIGIOUS SENTIMENT IN OPPOSITION TO ANARCHY, BUT THIS TEMPTATION IS AS ALLURING AS IT IS FALSE, BECAUSE MAN CAN ONLY AFFIRM HIS BEING BY ACCEPTING REALITY AND HIS OWN PLACE WITHIN IT. THIS, HOWEVER, MEANS ACCEPTING A REALITY WHICH DOESN'T HAPPEN ON ITS OWN. TRUTH, BEAUTY

INTRODUCTION The Time of the Soul

AND HAPPINESS ARE NEEDS WHICH HAVE BROUGHT MEN OF ALL RACES TO SEARCH FOR THEM ENERGETICALLY AND INCESSANTLY THROUGHOUT HISTORY. THESE ARE THE ASPIRATIONS THAT HAVE FUELLED AN INTENSE EXCHANGE OF IDEAS AMONG THE PEOPLE OF THE WORLD. IF THERE IS ANY HUMAN EXPERIENCE WHICH IS COMPARABLE IN TIME AND IN SPACE, IT IS THE RELIGIOUS EXPERIENCE, EVEN THOUGH IT IS EXPRESSED AND REALIZED IN DIFFERENT AND EVEN, OPPOSING, WAYS. CEREMONIES RICH IN POMP ARE PRESENT IN EVERY BELIEF SYSTEM, WHETHER IT IS AN ORGANISED RELIGION, AN ESOTERIC CULT OR A TRIBAL TRADITION. THEY ARE EXPRESSED THROUGHOUT THE WORLD IN FORMS WHICH INCLUDE RHYTHMIC PRAYER AND HYPNOTIC DANCE OR, WHICH

The Time of the Soul

SIMPLY CONSIST OF MEDITATION, CONTEMPLATION OR CONCENTRATION. THESE METHODS, EVEN IN THEIR APPARENT DIVERSITY, SHARE A SINGLE GOAL: TO GAIN AWARENESS OF THE GREAT UNKNOWN. THEY HAVE LAID THE FOUNDATIONS OF HISTORY AND THEY ARE AT THE VERTIGINOUS PEAK OF OUR REASONING. MAN SEEKS, DURING THE LIMITED SPACE OF HIS OWN HORIZON, THE PRESENCE OF AN ABSOLUTE, AND OFTEN ENDS UP IDENTIFYING IT WITH HIS OWN IMAGE OR WITH AN INFINITE SERIES OF IDOLS. THE MYSTERY OF DIVINE REVELATION MARKS THE FINITE NATURE OF HUMAN LIFE AND CLOAKS US IN DIGNITY.

401 • Peru. A candle's uncertain light reveals a deep meditation.

402-403 • China. A monk's intense look introduces us to the spiritual contents of the Tankas behind his back. Painted on canvas or on gesso, the Tankas are deep and colorful symbols of his faith.

404 • China. A faithful Tibetan manifests his belief by prostrating himself
on the pavement of the Potala, the fortress monastery of Lhasa.

405 • China. An elderly man recites a sutra, a Tibetan prayer, accompanying
it with the movement of his Prayer Wheel.

China. Two Buddhist monks, a youth and an old man, live their days immersed in reading and meditation.

China. Between the young aspiring Tibetan monks, the last in line yields to a moment of distraction.

410-411 • Bhutan. A group of monks participate in the celebration of the Tashicho Dzong during the Thimpu Festival.

411 • Bhutan. A monk observes the celebration of the Tashicho Dzong, during the Thimpu Festival.

• Bhutan. Two moments of a Cham, which is a religious masked dance, during the Paro Tsechu Festival. During these celebrations the Dzong (the fortified monasteries) are open for the public.

414 and 414-415 ● India. A Hindu Holy Man practices yoga on the shores of the Ganges in Gaumukh.

416-417 ● India. During the Kumbha Mela, the ritual mass purification that occurs in the sacred Ganges, these people have congregated in Prayag.

418-419 and 419 ● India. During the Kumbha Mela the Hindu Holy Men are the first to dive in the Ganges.

420-421 ● The Khumba Mela is held every three years in 4 different cities and attracts more than ten million believers. This picture was taken in Prayag Allahabad.

422-423 ● India. A Hindu Holy Man in Rajasthan grants the photographer a few moments of his meditative life.

423 ● India. Purification in sacred waters is a fundamental ritual of Hinduism.

Singapore. Two instants of the rich and colorful Hindu Thaipusam procession, which, once a year, crosses Little India. Costumes, flower decorations of every type and, in some cases, self-harming behavior characterize the celebration's most vibrant moments.

Indonesia, on the island of Bali. Women from the village of Mas carry their offerings for the traditional Harvest feast.

428-429 • Japan. Fire and music are recurring elements in the Kagura celebrations.

429 • Korea. A traditional wedding, according to the Confucian religion, follows very ancient rituals.

430-431 • China. Inside a pagoda, bundles of incense sticks perfume the air and create an atmosphere favorable for prayer.

Vietnam. A woman wearing a traditional Ao Dai costume in the Giac Lam pagoda in Saigon.

433

434 • Thailand. Two young monks
chat in front of a temple
in Phuket.

434-435 • Thailand. Prayer is undertaken
around a gigantic statue
of a reclined Buddha.

436-437 • Libya. A Muslim prays in
the desert towards of the Mecca.

438-439 • India. Neatly and rigorously
separated, men and women pray
in a mosque.

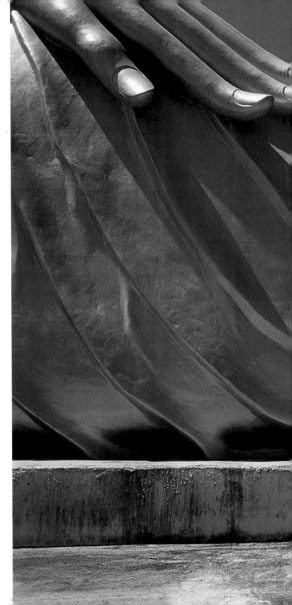

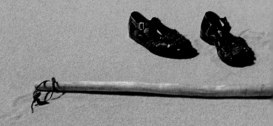

440 • Saudi Arabia. Every year, large crowds of Muslims make a pilgrimage to Mecca. The Black Stone is considered by Muslims to be the last fragment of the heavenly "ancient home" destroyed during the great flood.

441 • Saudi Arabia. An infinite line of pilgrims hold out their hands towards the gilded door of the Kaaba.

442 • Saudi Arabia. A Muslim, having arrived from distant Nigeria, prays at the door of the Prophet's Mosque in Medina.

443 • Saudi Arabia. A group of Indian women on a pilgrimage from Kerala, invoke the benevolence of the Prophet in Medina.

Senegal. A faithful subject joins his hands in prayer in front of the Sheik Ahmadou Bamba's tomb in Touba.

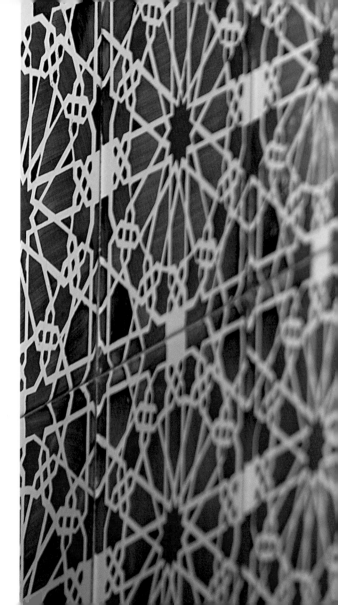

Israel. The Jewish rite of the Bar Mitzvah is celebrated in front of the Wailing Wall in Jerusalem.

Israel. Men praying at the Wailing Wall in Jerusalem, one of the most sacred places of Jewish religion.

450-451 • Israel. A crowd of pilgrims carry the cross along the Via Dolorosa in Jerusalem.

451 • Israel. The patriarch leads the Palm Sunday procession to the basilica of the Holy Sepulcher in Jerusalem.

452 • Spain. A "penitente" (penitent)
walks in a Good Friday procession in Seville.

452-453 • Spain. The "penitentes"
(penitents) carry crosses during one of the
processions which are undertaken in Seville
during the Holy Week.

454 • Spain. The members of a brotherhood walk in a nocturnal procession during Holy Week in Seville.

455 • France. The most important religious celebrations present the occasion to wear exquisite traditional clothes.

456 • Italy. A statue of the Virgin Mary is carried on shoulders by the faithful during the Easter processions in Sardinia.

456-457 • Italy. The celebrations for the passion of Christ arrive at their apex during the Good Friday procession in Sicily.

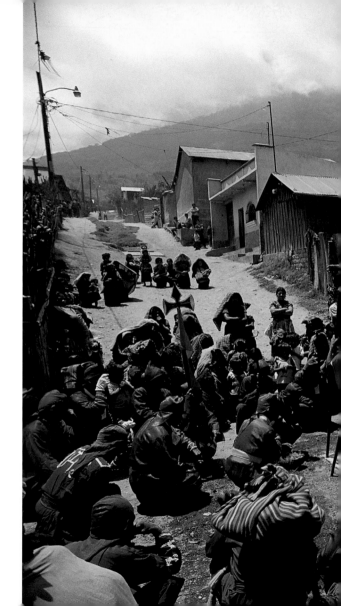

Guatemala. Men wearing ancient Roman attire carry a representation of the Passion of Christ in Quiche.

460 • Guatemala. The faithful pray around the flower and incense offerings in the church of San Andrés Sajcabajá in Quiche.

461 • Guatemala. The faithful pray on top of the Nueve Sillas in Totonicapàn, and then descend to the bottom of the gorge.

Peru. Two moments of the popular Qoyllur Rit'i (snow star) festival in the heart of the Andes.

● Peru. Faith can bring about the climbing of mountains, as with these believers who participated in the quest for Qoyllur Rit'i, which according to popular belief, is buried within the mountain.

● Ivory Coast. The mask allows those who wear it to assume another identity, like that of an ancestor or of a divinity.

Mali. The complex Dogon universe is perfectly expressed in the rich symbology present in their dances and disguises.

Kenya. Two Masai warriors paint their chests in order to prepare their bodies for a ceremony.

472-473 ● Kenya. The rites of passage, the ceremonies which accompany the most important moments in the growth of an individual within the tribe, are celebrated in the Masai society with spectacular dances.

473 ● Kenya. The Samburus adopt explosive forms of dances during their celebrations.

The PLEASURES of FOOD

Guatemala. A woman cooks a typical maize tortilla on the wood fire in her home.

INTRODUCTION The Pleasures of Food

Since the beginning, all human groups have explored the world by tasting it in an adventure which knows no end. Beyond food solely as a means of survival, rituals have been constructed which attribute an irreplaceable social importance to the "table." Man has chosen to eat his meals with his fellows because he wants and needs to affirm his sense of belonging to a society and to a family. The table, in this sense, is first of all a meeting place where individuals communicate with each other and where they learn about the world. Sometimes, business is conducted at the table and, at other times, love or hate flare. According to an Italian proverb, "One never gets old at the table"

INTRODUCTION The Pleasures of Food

ROUND TABLES, ELEGANTLY SET, ARE THE STUFF OF KINGS AND EMPERORS WHILE SUPPERS AND BANQUETS EVOKE BIBLICAL FEASTS. IN FACT, THE TABLE AND THE SHARING OF FOOD IS THE BACKDROP FOR THE MOST CELEBRATED MOMENTS IN OUR HISTORY. JESUS CHOSE A BANQUET FOR THE PERFORMANCE OF HIS FIRST MIRACLE, AND GAVE HIS LAST TESTAMENT WHILE SITTING AT A TABLE, AT HIS LAST SUPPER, SURROUNDED BY HIS DISCIPLES AROUND HIM. DYNASTIES ARE FOUNDED AT THE TABLE AND, IT COULD BE TRUE THAT THE ASTUTE KING SOLOMON – THANKS TO THE EFFECTS OF A RICH MEAL – SUCCEEDED IN WINNING THE BEAUTIFUL QUEEN OF SHEBA. EATING ISN'T ALWAYS THE MAIN OBJECTIVE OF SITTING AT A TABLE. SOMETIMES, IT'S MORE THE JOY OF CELEBRATING A NEW BIRTH OR A WED-

The Pleasures of Food
Introduction

DING. AT OTHER TIMES, IT'S THE DEATH OF A LOVED ONE WHICH REUNITES FRIENDS AND RELATIVES AROUND A TABLE. PEOPLE ALSO SIT AROUND A TABLE TO CLOSE IMPORTANT AGREEMENTS OR JUST TO CONNECT WITH EACH OTHER. EVER MORE FREQUENTLY IN OUR SOCIETY, WE IDENTIFY THE PLEASURES OF THE TABLE WITH CULTURE, ART AND LITERATURE. SOME WRITERS SAY THAT EATING AT A GOOD RESTAURANT IS THE BEST WAY TO CHEER UP OR TO SUBLIMATE ONE'S PASSIONS WHILE INEBRIATED WITH THE OFFER OF DELICIOUS FOODS. WRITER VAZQUEZ MONTALBAN, HOWEVER, LAMENTED: "I'D LIKE TO HAVE A LITTLE OF EVERYTHING, EVEN THOUGH I'D NEVER LIVE LONG ENOUGH TO TASTE ALL OF IT."

● Denmark. A little boy curiously tastes a kebab.

Canada. An Inuit woman cooks seal meat inside her igloo in Churchill, Manitoba.

Norway. During spring migration, the Sami tribe eat their meals around the fire lit in their tents.

Germany. A woman photographed cooking in the pantry.

Italy. The risotto is one of the traditional dishes in Vercelli.

488 ● France. A seller prepares
a gigantic pot of potatoes in
the Bastille market in Paris.

488-489 ● Switzerland. Skillful hands
prepare a seasoned cheese (Raclette),
which will be eaten piping hot.

Italy. The art of preparing pizza, now a world renowned dish, finds real artists in the city of Naples.

France. The elaborate recipes of French cuisine are handed down and spread in top-quality academies.

Italy. A cook prepares various varieties of pasta in a restaurant in Positano.

Ethiopia. Two instants of the preparation of injera, the typical bread eaten by the populations in the plateaus.

498 • Kenya. A child eats his meal directly from the bowl. It usually consists of a mixture of water and wheat flour.

499 • Mali. A small boy eats a large slice of watermelon with great pleasure, it is an important source of water and sugar.

500-501 • Ethiopia. A woman of
Bume ethnicity prepares a meal
for her family in the village of Mer,
in the region of Omo.

501 • Burkina Faso. The task
of preparing food for the entire
family often falls on the
elder women.

• Egypt. In her camp in
the peninsula of Sinai, a Bedouin
woman slowly prepares
the cardamom, a grain spice
used to perfume both
coffee and tea.

5 KGS NET WEIGHT

PURE EDIBLE VEGETABLE OIL

MADE IN HOLLAND BY

ROTTERDAMSCHE MARGARINE INDUSTRY
ROMI B.Z.   VLAARDINGEN

Holland

India. A Changpas woman in Ladakh cooks meat in a sort of pressure cooker, while cornbread cooks in the stove.

● China. A Buddhist pilgrim heading towards Mount Kailas, in Tibet, gets ready to eat his meal surrounded by breathtaking scenery.

● China. Although Chinese cuisine is slowly gaining ground, meals, in the most isolated places in Tibet, still consist of millet, meat and dairy products. The Tsampa (being prepared in the picture) is the main food (roasted barley flour, often mixed with salty butter tea). Yogurt and dried, boiled or smoked yak and mutton meat are also very popular.

Afghanistan.
A peddler offers
his delicacies in the
streets of Kabul.

● Uzbekistan. Two
elders of Bukhara
prepare a beverage
for a rich banquet.
The Plov, the Uzbek
version of pilaf,
is the main local dish.
It consists
of fried and boiled
meat, onions, carrots
and rice with raisins,
chickpeas or fruit.

514 and 515 ● India. The preparation of traditional food and beverages is a domestic task reserved exclusively for the women of Rajasthan.

516-517 ● India. The preparation and vending of sweets occurs outside in this Pushar bazaar in Rajasthan.

518-519 ● China. In the vegetable market of Shanghai a cook is preparing a meal based on a mixture of steam-cooked flour.

519 ● China. The art of hand preparing pasta is a thousand-year old Chinese tradition.

China. A restaurant's old cook, in Chengdu, displays all his skills in making noodles.

● China. A cook
in the market of
Kemsat gets ready
to remove dozens
of identical portions
from the oven.

Vietnam. Some women supervise the preparation of the soy pudding "Che Ko." With rice, combined with several vegetables or fish, it is one of the traditional Vietnamese dishes.

526 ● Thailand. A woman cooks on board her boat in the floating market of Damnoen Saduak.

526-527 ● Vietnam. In the floating market of Phung Miep, food is served on board boats.

Myanmar. A group of young monks prepare to eat their meal in a monastery in Mandalay.

China. Even in the Chinese metropolis, chopsticks are much more widely used than western cutlery. In China five types of cuisine exist, each one tied to a particular region. Cantonese is the most popular of the cuisines throughout the rest of the world.

United States.
Cooks from all over
the world come to
New York to learn the
secrets of new and
creative cuisine.

534 and 535 • Japan. Fish and raw food are some of the most prominent characteristics of Japanese cuisines.

536-537 • Japan. All the richness and variety of traditional Japanese cuisine can be appreciated in this restaurant in Tokyo.

538-539 ● Brazil. A chef personally handles his recipe's preparation in a restaurant's kitchen in Sao Paolo.

540 ● United States. A man carefully prepares his barbeque in his garden in San Rafael, California.

540-541 ● United States. Two members of a voluntary association prepare a barbeque in Greenwood, Delaware.

542 • United States. A chef observes the cooking process of a foie gras (goose liver) based dish.

542-543 • United States. Meals based on fish and shellfish abound in restaurants in Boston.

544 • United States. Eating a large slice of watermelon in the company of others enhances a pleasurable warm summer afternoon.

545 • United States. A woman proudly shows the apple pies she placed on the window sill to cool.

Mexico. A woman cooks her country's typical recipes in a market stand in Jalisco, Guadalajara.

STREETS
Across the
WORLD
of the

● Peru. Waiting for a train and the journey in its crowded carriages are both a meeting and a trading occasion for the people of the Andes.

INTRODUCTION Across the Streets of the World

Man has always seen travel as a metaphor for life. Both our ancestral consciousness and our modern awareness tell us that travel and traveling are genuine representations of existence, like a long cord stretched throughout the arc of our earthly experience. Only at death does our voyage end. Often in our modern frenzy we are too quick to consume the present, because our focus is on the future; but we really should remember that the end of one chapter is the beginning of another. The history of mankind is a voyage, a round-trip with a happy ending, like many stories from classic. It is a straight line with no fixed destination. Contemporary authors create characters where horizons

INTRODUCTION Across the Streets of the World

ARE LIMITLESS. FOR ALL OF US, HOWEVER, THE ACT OF TRAVELING IS THE DESTINATION, AN UNKNOWN ONE CLOAKED IN VARIOUS AND SOMETIMES CONTRADICTORY MEANINGS. TODAY, WE TRAVEL TO ESCAPE, TO BREAK A PATTERN AND TO DISCOVER OUR TRUE ESSENCE. THE PO-LITICAL AND CULTURAL BORDERS WE CROSS – AND THE PERSONAL ONES, TOO, ACCORDING TO OUR PHYSICAL ABIL-ITIES – ARE THERE TO BE OVERCOME. WE TRAVEL TO FEEL AT HOME IN THE WORLD, TO GO BEYOND THE COLUMNS OF HERCULES TO BECOME GUESTS AND WANDERERS AT THE SAME TIME. WHEN WE TRAVEL, WE DISCOVER THAT WE DON'T REALLY POSSESS ANYTHING, WE ONLY HAVE THINGS ON LOAN, WHETHER FOR A NIGHT OR FOR A LIFETIME. THIS PERTAINS TO EVERYTHING WE TOUCH AND EVEN TO WHERE

Across the Streets of the World

Introduction

WE LIVE. TRAVELING MEANS BEING AN OBSERVER, A CURIOUS ACCOMPLICE TO A DIFFERENT REALITY. LIVING AND TRAVELING ARE THE SAME THING BECAUSE A VOYAGE – AS WELL AS BEING IN SPACE – IS ALWAYS A VOYAGE IN TIME, TOO. TO THOSE WHO ARE IMMERSED IN THIS INFINITE TRIP, IT MIGHT SERVE TO REMEMBER BORGE'S PARABLE ABOUT THE MAN WHO WANTED TO DESIGN THE WORLD AND WHO, THROUGH THE YEARS, INCLUDES MOUNTAINS, RIVERS, STARS AND PEOPLE IN HIS VISION, BUT FINDS – JUST BEFORE DYING – THAT THIS PATIENTLY CONSTRUCTED LABYRINTH OF LINES ACTUALLY TRACES THE IMAGE OF HIS OWN FACE.

553 • Nigeria. A truck overloaded with men and goods confronts a difficult journey in the sandy desert.

554-555 • Niger. Camel caravans are the only possible way to transport large cargos across the Sahara.

556 ● Mali. Two Tuareg,
in the middle of sand clouds,
lead the dromedary caravans
in the desert.

556-557 ● Mali. Some Tuareg
nomads give water to their cattle
in the Sahara desert.

Egypt. Village dwellers still travel by camel, just as they did two thousand years ago.

560-561 • China. Traveling with only one mount, monks leave the village to return to their praying place.

562-563 • Morocco. Snow does not surprise the inhabitants of Magdaz in their transits along the Tessaout valley.

564-565 • Mozambique. Three fishermen cross the Malawi lake on board a canoe made of bulrushes and intertwined bark.

The Democratic Republic of Congo. Aligned in a narrow canoe, a group of Pygmies glide into the heart of the equatorial forest.

Tanzania. Oblivious to the heavy summer rains, two boys move with their cart in a Zanzibar market.

570-571 • Kenya. The region's scarce water resources force the Turkana people to a rigid social administration of the few existing wells.

572-573 • Turkey. Early in the morning, the women of the Goreme Valley in Cappadocia arrive to work in the fields.

574-575 • Vietnam. A woman crosses a river over a suspended bridge.

576-577 • Nepal. Long rows of praying flags accompany travelers and protect them on even the most dangerous of paths.

578 ● India. A fragile rope bridge is often the only way that allows the inhabitants
of Ladakh to cross the rivers.

579 ● China. Dangerously holding on to a rope, four men cross a river
in Lamping, Yunnan.

China. Two youths head towards the nearest market after having loaded their goods on Tibet's cheapest and most widespread means of transport: the yak.

582 • China. Hand in hand, a little boy and an old man get ready to cross a mountain
river in Tibet thanks to a solid wooden bridge.

583 • China. Firmly leading his animal, a man completes the crossing
of a wooden bridge on the Dajin Chuan river.

584 • India. A flower seller paddles slowly in the calm waters of a channel flowing from the Dal lake in Kashmir.

585 • Myanmar. The population living on the shores of the Inle lake has developed a skillful paddling technique which permits them to predominantly use their lower limbs.

586-587 • India. A man transports tourists on the Yamuna river in Agra.

587 • India. A family seeks salvation on a small raft during one of the periodical floods which hit the southern parts of the country.

588-589 • Cambodia. A train crosses, with difficulty, the country's plains carrying an improbably assorted load.

590-591 and 591 ● India. All means of transport are utilized to carry is used to transport agricultural products, from fresh milk to simple potable water.

592-593 ● India. A caravan of oxen-pulled wagons move slowly in the village's agricultural countryside.

Myanmar.
The unusual encounter
of two traditional and
very different means
of transport in a
street of the Indian
sub-continent.

596 ● Malaysia. The traditional rickshaw continues to be a very popular means of transport in the large Asian metropolis.

597 ● Vietnam. A parent accompanies his children to school along a street which crosses the Da river's valley.

Nepal. An incredible endurance against fatigue, combined with perfect adaptation
to great heights, allow even the oldest members of the Sherpa population
to carry heavy loads across long trails.

600 • Myanmar. A clever solution allows this woman to carry her son and a basket full of food at the same time.

601 • China. A man heads towards the Chengdu market in the region of Sichuan.

602-603 • Vietnam. A group of motorcycles waits for the green light in Hanoi.

604-605 • Hong Kong. A bus traverses the Asian metropolis.

606 • Japan. A boy moves deftly across a junction of cycle tracks
in Tamagawa Avenue, Tokyo.

607 • Hong Kong. A young delivery man crosses a large junction in Chatham road.

608-609 • Russia. A man watches the world go by from the window of the bus in Moscow.

610 • Vietnam. Two women, wrapped in their *ao dai,* cross Ho Chi Minh City.

611 • Holland. The bicycle remains the predominant means of travel
in the Netherlands.

612-613 • Germany. A cyclist rides on a beautiful country road along the shores
of the Danube.

614-615 • Canada. A sleigh, hauled by three horses, crosses the snow-covered forest.

616-617 • Norway. In winter, Laplanders are able to move from one place to another thanks to the help of strong reindeers.

618-619 • Norway. Proudly sitting behind his master, a Husky dog braves the journey by bike in the cold of Lapponia.

Romania. A Rom family faces an endless journey in the countryside of old Europe.

Ireland. A timeless picture: a coach crosses the fairy-tale landscape of the Irish countryside.

624 and 625 • United States. The Amish, in Pennsylvania, continue to use traditional means of transport, both open or closed carriages, ignoring the rush of our times.

626-627 • France. A long queue of cars patiently awaits the arrival of the low tide to be able to reach a small island on the Atlantic Coast.

For

TRADITION

for JOY

China. An opera singer from Beijing applies the final touches to her make-up before going back to the scene.

INTRODUCTION For Tradition, for Joy

"WHAT IS A RITE?" ASKED THE LITTLE PRINCE. "THEY ARE ACTIONS TOO OFTEN NEGLECTED," SAID THE FOX. "THEY ARE WHAT MAKE ONE DAY DIFFERENT FROM ANOTHER, ONE HOUR DIFFERENT FROM OTHER HOURS. THERE IS A RITE, FOR EXAMPLE, AMONG MY HUNTERS. EVERY THURSDAY THEY DANCE WITH THE VILLAGE GIRLS. SO THURSDAY IS A WONDERFUL DAY FOR ME! I CAN TAKE A WALK AS FAR AS THE VINEYARDS. BUT IF THE HUNTERS DANCED AT JUST ANY TIME, EVERY DAY WOULD BE THE SAME, AND I SHOULD NEVER HAVE ANY VACATION AT ALL." MAN HAS THE NEED FOR CERE-MONIES AND RITUALS TO GIVE DEPTH AND SIGNIFI-CANCE TO EVENTS AND TO PRESERVE THEM FOR ETER-NITY AND WREST THEM FROM THE MORTAL DESTINY OF

INTRODUCTION For Tradition, for Joy

HUMAN THINGS. FOR THIS REASON, EVERY SELF-RE-SPECTING INDIVIDUAL, FAMILY OR GROUP EMPHASIZES THE MOST IMPORTANT MOMENTS OF EXISTENCE WITH FESTIVE OR SOLEMN CEREMONIES. WEARING NEW CLOTHES OR EATING SOMETHING SPECIAL ACQUIRES DEEP SIGNIFICANCE AND MARKS THE RHYTHM OF PASS-ING TIME GIVING A DIFFERENT TASTE TO DAILY LIFE. ON-LY A FEW GESTURES ARE NEEDED TO TRANSFORM ANY MOMENT INTO A FESTIVITY: WHERE SMALL OBJECTS ARE MAGICALLY TRANSFORMED INTO SACRED SYM-BOLS AND WHERE A DREAMLIKE AURA PERVADES NON-DESCRIPT TIME. IN THE RHYTHMIC BEAT OF LIFE, WED-DING CEREMONIES HOLD A SPECIAL PLACE BOTH FOR THE COUPLE INVOLVED AND FOR THE COMMUNITY. AS

For Tradition, for Joy

Introduction

SUCH, WEDDING CEREMONIES ARE CELEBRATED IN A SOLEMN RESPECTFUL WAY BUT THEY ARE ALSO FILLED WITH GAIETY AND JOYFULNESS. IN MANY SOCIETIES, FAMILIES INVEST HUGE RESOURCES AND ENERGIES INTO WEDDING CEREMONIES TO ESTABLISH OR CONSOLIDATE ALLIANCES, TO INCREASE THEIR OWN WEALTH AND, NATURALLY, TO SEAL A VERY IMPORTANT CONTRACT WITH LIFE. ALL COUPLES SEEK A BETTER FUTURE AFTER THEIR WEDDINGS BECAUSE THEY KNOW THAT ONLY THE EXCLUSIVE LOVE OF ANOTHER HUMAN BEING CAN MAKE THE JOY OF A WEDDING LAST A LIFETIME.

• Papua New Guinea. Body care and facial decorations are quite widespread in various New Guinea populations.

634 • Morocco. A group of Berber women wear the veil on their wedding day.

634-635 • Morocco. Some young Imichil couples wait for their wedding ceremony.

636 • Tunisia. The bride's gown (red – an auspicious color) must be weaved in gold .

636-637 • Tunisia. The wedding day is called *djefa*, from the name of the chair which, bound on the back of a dromedary, carries the bride.

● Morocco.
A young bride,
surrounded by guests,
wears a gown rich
with decorations and
precious fabrics.

640 ● Morocco. Wearing the traditional djellaba, a group of men get ready to dance in the Rose Festival.

640-641 ● Morocco. Standing in front of the men, the women exhibit their elaborate traditional clothes in the Rose Festival's dances.

Niger. The smile of the young Bororos
hides the secret, the magic and the
hypnotic charm of the Gerewol ritual.

643

Nigeria. During the Durban festival, the population wears traditional costumes during horse parades to celebrate the end of Ramadan.

Kenya. Proud of their exuberant ornaments, Samburu men and women prepare to dance, performing very high jumps and rhythmically moving their necks.

Namibia. With their bodies entirely covered with red earth, the Himba let themselves go in whirling dances with the simple clapping of hands acting as rhythm.

● China. Under a storm-
threatening sky, Tibetan women
display their splendid traditional
clothes covered with jewels (left)
or dance (right) wearing their
ample clothes with
puffed-sleeves.

China. On the occasion of the Yaji, the festival of summer pleasures in Litang, Tibet, horsemen compete in various ability challenges including archery (left) and races (right).

● Mongolia. Every year the
anniversary of the Mongol
revolution is celebrated with the
Naadam Festival and a spectacular
horse race. Amongst the
traditional competitions are
archery (left) and wrestling (right).

South Korea. Simulating the movements made by natural elements, dozens of dancers perform in the Sina Festival in Gyeongju.

China. Girls of all ages of the Miao ethnicity sing in their traditional costumes in Anshun in the province of Guizhou.

China. The flower dance festival is a tradition of the Miao people in the region of Guizhou.

662 • China. In Hong Kong, during the Chinese New Year Celebration, a great feast with dancing and parades in traditional costumes is organized.

663 • Japan. The clothes of the Heian period are worn by girls during the traditional celebration of Hojo Godai Matsuri, with the procession of warriors in Odawara.

664 ● Taiwan. The ancient ritual of the Lion Dance is performed in a square in Taipei.

664-665 ● China. A young artist performs in the celebrations for the arrival of the Chinese New Year in Beijing.

China. Two actors from the Beijing National Opera prepare their theatrical masks before going on stage. Contrary to other theatrical traditions, in Beijing's opera both men and women perform on stage, and the switching of roles and masks between them is not unusual.

668 ● China. An intense picture caught on stage, of an actor in the National Opera in Beijing.

668-669 ● Great Britain. Artists at Beijing's National Opera stage "The Legend of the Serpent" in a London theatre.

670 and 670-671 • China. A show from Beijing's Dancing School and a spectacular performance for the spectators in which colors and traditional costumes complete the harmony of the movements.

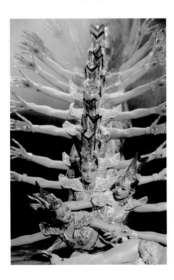

672-673 • India. During the Pooram Festival in Kerala a grand procession is performed of thirty Indian elephants which, harnessed and decorated with umbrellas and fans, perform with circle around the temple accompanied by music.

- India. Associated with the God Krishna, the arrival of spring is celebrated by Hindus with an overwhelming bath of water and colorful powder called *gunal*.

India. Men, women and children compete in throwing powder or colored water at each other which represent the colors of spring during the Holi Festival.

678 • India. Some of the faithful, painted in the sacred colors, are pictured during the celebrations in honor of the god Krishna in Rajasthan.

678-679 • India. A Hindu lets himself be dragged in a suggestive red tide during the celebrations for the coming of spring.

India. A Kathakali dancer refines his make-up (left) before performing as an actor (right) in a show in Trivandrum in Kerala.

682 and 682-683 ● Indonesia, Bali Island. Some dancers perform the traditional Legong dance displaying perfect control of their movements and facial expressions.

684-685 ● Myanmar. Paddling with legs on narrow and very crowded canoes, the inhabitants of the Inle Lake celebrate an important religious occurrence.

• Japan. The Jidai Matsuri is celebrated in Kyoto with a large parade where participants wear costumes which commemorate different historical periods.

● Japan. The complex make-up and the donning clothes which precede a display of Kabuki: to the left, the actor is preparing his make-up and, right, he enhances his mask with a wig.

690-691 and 691 ● Japan. Two acting companies are involved in the traditional and intense theatrical art of the Kabuki, which originates back to the end of the XVI century.

692-693 ● Japan. A group of Chiban youths carry the Mikoshi to sea – they are little temples mounted on special stretchers – during the Hadaka Matsuri. Water will purify the sanctuaries and the faithful from bad spirits.

Papua New Guinea. Body and facial decorations are very important for the Papuan people especially during the festival on Mount Hagen.

Germany. The Theresienwiese park in Munich every year becomes the favorite destination for beer enthusiasts from all over Europe during the Oktoberfest.

Germany. The clash between valiant horsemen is the most intense moment of the medieval horse tournament of Kaltenberg.

● Italy. The equestrian exhibitions which are performed on the streets of Oristano constitute the fulcrum of the Sartiglia celebration in Sardinia.

Spain. The raging bulls on the streets of Pamplona continue to be a very important feature of the feast of San Firmino.

Spain. A group of flamenco dancers parade wearing traditional costume (left) and perform (right) during the "Feria di Siviglia."

Spain. In Seville during the annual
"feria" there is a mixture of all the
elements of the Andalucian folklore –
bullfights, flamenco and
masked parades.

708-709 • France. The "castellers" get ready to form a human tower in Perpignan, according to an ancient Catalan tradition.

709 • France. The human tower has formed, it is six levels high and forms one of the "Castells" of Catalan history.

• Ireland. The feast of St. Patrick, on the March 17th, brings the Irish people to the squares where, with parades and costumes in traditional colors, they celebrate their patron saint.

United States. The costumes of pilgrims, turkeys and a gigantic Spider-Man parade in the streets of New York during the Thanksgiving Day parade.

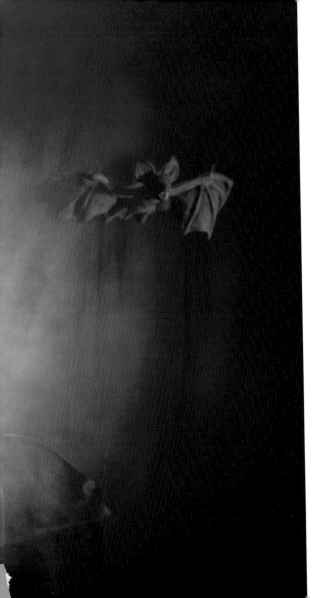

● United States. During
Halloween the world of the dead
is evoked through shows,
disguises and theme parties.

716 • United States. A child picks up a pumpkin to celebrate Halloween. With the immigration of the Irish to America the orange vegetable has become the symbol of Halloween, substituting the traditional turnip.

716-717 • United States. Halloween is also a celebration dedicated to children who, disguised, parade the neighborhood streets "Trick or Treating."

718 ● United States. An allegorical wagon invites the spectators to the fun during the carnival of New Orleans.

718-719 ● Trinidad. The magic of fire and the pleasure of wearing a costume are the ingredients of this Caribbean carnival.

● Brazil. The popular carnival parades
of Rio De Janeiro, which are held in the
sambodrome area of the city, are one
of the most extraordinary spectacles
of the world.

Peru. The Qoyllur Rit'i is the most important pilgrimage of Latin America. On the Holy Trinity Day, pilgrims from Ocongate (Cusco), some masquerading as Andean mythical characters, climb up to the edge of the perennial snows.

Peru. Two moments from the festival of
Raqchi, in which the Andean population
perform their traditional dances.

Peru. Masked dancers perform during the celebration of the Qoyllur Rit'i in the Cordillera Vilcanota.

AUTHORS Biographies

INDEX

■ VALERIA MANFERTO DE FABIANIS

She is the editor of the series. Valeria Manferto De Fabianis was born in Vercelli, Italy and studied arts at the Università Cattolica del Sacro Cuore in Milan, graduating with a degree in philosophy.

She is an enthusiastic traveler and nature lover. She has collaborated on the production of television documentaries and articles for the most prestigious Italian specialty magazines and has also written many photography books.

She co-founded Edizioni White Star in 1984 with Marcello Bertinetti and is the editorial director.

■ FABRIZIO FINETTI

was born in Siena in 1960. Photographer and journalist, he quickly transposed his passion for travel into valuable reportages. In 1992 he started a long foreign working experience, first in Greece, then in Ethiopia, and finally in Argentina. He works with several Italian travel magazines. Since 2003 he works and lives in Barcelona and as from 2004 he collaborates in the Spanish agency AISA Media. He has worked for years with White Star Editions, publishing house for which he produced the volume Barcelona.

PHOTO CREDITS

PHOTO CREDITS

PHOTO CREDITS

Pages 456 and 456-457 Giulio Veggi/Archivio White Star

Pages 458-459, 460 and 461 Thomas Hoepker/Magnum Photos/Contrasto

Pages 462, 462-463, 464 and 464-465 Marcello Bertinetti/Archivio White Star

Pages 466-467 and 467 Charles & Josette Lenars/Corbis

Page 468 Patrick Syder/Lonely Planet Images

Pages 468-469 Michel Renaudeau/Agefotostock/Marka

Pages 470-471 Roger De La Harpe; Gallo Images/Corbis

Pages 472-473 Sue Cunningham/DanitaDelimont.com

Page 473 Michel Denis-Huot/Hoa-qui/HachettePhotos/Contrasto

Page 475 Thomas Hoepker/Magnum Photos/Contrasto

Page 479 Stuart Pearce/Agefotostock/Marka

Pages 480-481 Cindy Miller Hopkins/DanitaDelimont.com

Pages 482-483 and 483 B&C Alexander/NHPA/Photoshot

Pages 484-485 Barth/laif/Contrasto

Pages 486-487 Marcello Bertinetti/Archivio White Star

Page 488 Martin Moos/Lonely Planet Images

Pages 488-489 Sandro Vannini/Corbis

Pages 490-491 Atlantide Phototravel/Corbis

Pages 492-493 and 493 Pierre Vauthey/Corbis Sygma/Corbis

Pages 494-495 Vittoriano Rastelli/Corbis

Page 496 Frances Linzee Gordon/Lonely Planet Images

Page 497 Jim Sugar/Corbis

Page 498 Liba Taylor/Corbis

Page 499 Dan Herrick/Lonely Planet Images

Pages 500-501 Janis Miglav/DanitaDelimont.com

Page 501 DeAgostini/Getty Images

Page 502 Giulio Andreini/Agefotostock/Marka

Pages 502-503 Antonio Attini/Archivio White Star

Pages 504-505 Alison Wright/Corbis

Pages 506-507 Galen Rowell/Corbis

Pages 508 and 509 Tiziana and Gianni Baldizzone

Pages 510-511 Hahn/laif/Contrasto

Pages 512-513 Gueorgui Pinkhassov/Magnum Photos/Contrasto

Pages 514 and 515 Tiziana and Gianni Baldizzone/Archivio White Star

Pages 516-517 Jeremy Horner/Corbis

Pages 518-519 Stuart Franklin/Magnum Photos/Contrasto

Page 519 Wolf/laif/Contrasto

Pages 520-521 Bruno Barbey/Magnum Photos/Contrasto

Pages 522-523 David H. Wells/Corbis

Pages 524-525 Atlantide Phototravel/Corbis

Page 525 Mak Remissa/epa/Corbis

Page 526 John and Lisa Merrill/DanitaDelimont.com

Pages 526-527 Michael S. Yamashita/Corbis

Pages 528-529 Owen Franken/Corbis

Pages 530-531 and 531 Wolf/laif/Contrasto

Pages 532-533 Chien-Chi Chang/Magnum Photos/Contrasto

Page 534 James Marshall/Corbis

Page 535 Dallas & John Heaton/Agefotostock/Marka

Pages 536-537 Harry Guyaert/Magnum Photos/Contrasto

Pages 538-539 Andrea Pistolesi/Getty Images

Page 540 Corbis

Pages 540-541 Kevin Fleming/Corbis

Page 542 Mascarussi/Corbis

Pages 542-543 Karen Kasmauski/Corbis

Page 544 Julie Habel/Corbis

Page 545 Steve Chenn/Corbis

Pages 546-547 Danny Lehman/Corbis

Page 549 Marcello Bertinetti/Archivio White Star

Page 553 Frans Lemmens/Getty Images

Pages 554-555 Bruno Zanzottera

Page 556 Kazuyoshi Nomachi

Pages 556-557 Charles & Josette Lenars/Corbis

Pages 558 and 559 Marcello Bertinetti/Archivio White Star

Pages 560-561 Steve McCurry/Magnum Photos/Contrasto

Pages 562-563 Bruno Barbey/Magnum Photos/Contrasto

Pages 564-565 Peter Turnley/Corbis

Pages 566-567 Yves Gellie

Pages 568-569 Per-Anders Petterson/Getty Images

Pages 570-571 Adrian Arbib/Corbis

Pages 572-573 Jonathan Balir/Corbis

Pages 574-575 Nevada Wier/Corbis

Pages 576-577 Fabiano Ventura

Page 578 Christophe Boisvieux/Corbis

Page 579 Michael S. Yamashita/Corbis

Pages 580-581 Christophe Boisvieux

Pages 582 and 583 Tiziana and Gianni Baldizzone

Page 584 Steve McCurry/Magnum Photos/Contrasto

Page 585 Hiroji Kubota/Magnum Photos/Contrasto

Pages 586-587 Remi Benali/Corbis

Pages 587 epa/Corbis

Pages 588-589 Michael S. Yamashita/Corbis

Pages 590-591 Tiziana and Gianni Baldizzone/Archivio White Star

Page 591 Christophe Boisvieux

Pages 592-593 Jagdish Agarwal/Corbis

Pages 594-595 Robert Van Der Hilst/Corbis

Page 596 Bob Krist/Corbis

Page 597 Stefano Amantini/Atlantide Photo Travel

Page 598 Steve McCurry/Magnum Photos/Contrasto

Page 599 Roman Soumar/Corbis

Page 600 Christophe Boisvieux/Corbis

Page 601 Tom Nebbia/Corbis

Pages 602-603 Christophe Boisvieux/Corbis

Pages 604-605 Charles O' Rear/Corbis

Pages 606 and 607 B.S.P.I./Corbis

Pages 608-609 Alessandro Castiglioni/Auraphoto

Page 610 Stuart Dee/Getty Images